Sacrificing For Success

By

Blessed Thabang Mobosi

i

Sacrificing For Success

Sacrificing For Success

Author Blessed Thabang Mobosi

Biography

Blessed Thabang Mobosi is a preacher, a Christian coach, a minister, a motivational speaker, a prolific author of several books and a mentor of number of people. He is the founder of a fellowship, a mentoring campaign by the name "Power & Authority Christian Fellowship of God International" (PACFOGI) and a Youth Evangelical campaign by the name of "Jesus Redemption Campaign". His role model is Dag Heward Mills. He believes that his calling is to become an Evangelist, and he is also pursuing a career in Retail and Wholesale Business Management.

Sacrificing For Success

In 2016 he wrote two books "Destiny is a Matter of Choice" and "The Power Of Determination", both published by William Jenkins, a Canadian editor and publisher. His third book, published in 2017, was "Steps to Success (A Key to Success Creativity)". He has three other books published in his name. This is his seventh one.

Blessed believes in the Solomonic wisdom that God has given him, in serving the need of his mentees and in spreading the knowledge he has acquired to make the world a better place.

He is presently studying Retail and Wholesale Business Management at Tshwane University of Technology, Pretoria, South Africa.

He has been invited to different places many times to act as a minister.

Sacrificing For Success

Written by

Blessed Thabang Mobosi

Telephone Numbers:

+27 61 953 9726

+27 78 506 5555

+27 72 875 6983

Email: Blessed.btm@gmail.com

Facebook Page: Author Blessed Thabang Mobosi

Web site:
http://amazon.com/author/blessedmobosi

Copyright © Blessed Thabang Mobosi 2018, 2019

Edited by William Jenkins, Canada

williamhenryjenkins@gmail.com

ISBN 978-0-6399345-5-6

Sacrificing For Success

Sacrificing For Success

Dedication

I dedicate this book to my creator the almighty God for the success of all his creations.

Secondly, I dedicate this book to Mr. William Jenkins, my publisher from Canada. Thanks for your free help in editing and publishing my books from the time I was in high school and could not afford any publisher. I am grateful .

Acknowledgements

I give my thanks to my friend Mr. Simon Ntini. Thanks for all the good advice I got from you.

To my wonderful parents Mr. Antony Mobosi and Mrs. Rosina Mothopane Mobosi: thanks for all your support. Your harvest in my success awaits you.

Sacrificing For Success

Sacrificing For Success

Contents

Sacrificing For Success

Sacrificing For Success

Introduction

It is the ideal goal for everyone to be successful in life.

The truth about success is that it is achieved by only those who are willing to pay the price for it. In our lives, where we are today is due to the effort we made to get the success for which we hoped. Our successful achievements are directly proportional to the effort and sacrifice we made to get our desired result.

Although success is something we all wish to have, we all have different definitions and views of what success really is.

What Is Success?

The Cambridge Advanced Learner's Dictionary defines success as "achieving the result wanted or hoped for". I define a successful state as being one where all the profit comes to you as the owner or possessor of assets. It is the state of having more than enough so that even if you give away some of your possessions, you do not feel the loss.

If your life does not affect other people, you're not yet successful. The truth about life is that if you're not living to fulfil your own dreams, you're living your life to help someone else fulfil their dreams and certainly making it easier for them. You are either working for them or indirectly investing in them while you gain less.

There is nothing wrong with being an employee. You should plan your life to move from being just an employee

Sacrificing For Success

into becoming someone who owns his or her own company or business in the same profession or career path.

Do you plan on going to work for those years only to earn a living, getting your pension fund, and then become a granny. Are you going to work for money just to earn a living and to achieve all the small goals you have? Goals like:

- Getting a degree
- Getting married
- Having kids
- Working
- Living in a comfortable zone
- Sending your children to school
- Getting old
- Retiring

I know most of us would say "no" to this question, but that may be all that you are achieving. Are you just living for a comfortable life; working to meet all your needs and wants? I suggest that you should crave for more, more significant goals, more success. Go beyond the mundane level. What you envision is what you will possess.

It is how much further you are willing to go in life that will determine your success. Success is a matter of choice and all in all a matter of sacrifice. Only those who are willing to pay the price of sacrifice in order to achieve more will be successful.

Sacrificing For Success

If you don't like the fruit, then change the seed. If you don't like what you're harvesting, then change what you're sowing. You get rewards based only on that for which you have worked.

I assure you that if you are living a life where you are labouring just to pay debts, you are living your life at a loss. No one who is always in debt has joy of contentment in what he has. The only things he thinks about are all the debts and the little amount of money in his bank account. No one can live joyously in that type of life. I think the best debt to incur is an investment that will bring money in. It costs money to make money. Don't live your life in debt simply working to pay for things that do not provide a return.

In essence, you are working for your bank rather than for yourself. Some of your increasing debts may be just to pay off earlier debts. You should strive to get to a position of being an investor instead of being a debtor. Then you will be gaining income interest, you will make more money, you will be able to spend some of your money and still have enough of everything without owing anybody.

There's nothing more joyful in life than having more than enough, being a lender instead of being a borrower, being a giver, not always a receiver. Don't live your life just to earn a living. Strive for more.

I've observed many people who want to have more money. They are just working normally and doing nothing to get more money. They simply expect to get more. It is

Sacrificing For Success

as though they are craving a miracle. That extra money that they want cannot just come out of thin air to them. It is impossible.

You can't expect a promotion when you've been sitting around with that ancient diploma for years. Upgrade your credentials to qualify for a promotion.

You can't wish to have a million in your bank account when you're receiving just a little and spending more than what you receive while doing nothing that can generate an increase in your income or financial possessions. Don't just wish. Do something extreme; do it to bring that extreme something into reality. Many people wish for more, but are not doing anything to bring it into a reality. Realise that things don't just happen; something has to be done in order to make things happen.

What Is Not Success?

Many people think if that if you go to university, get a degree and have a good job, you have success. I tell you that having a degree and a good job is not success; that's an achievement. You've achieved your degree and got a job. Congratulation on attaining that long-term goal; it is an achievement.

You realise that you are an employee and say you're successful. You are a worker, buddy. You're working for someone.

Sacrificing For Success

Maybe I should say, "You are working for someone to help them fulfil their dreams and goals. You're helping them to become more successful".

As long as you're working for someone and the whole profit goes to them and you get only a share of the profit (salary), you're not yet successful. You're still in the process of becoming successful. It is up to you to sacrifice the little that you have in order to start something that will convert you into being a successful person. It is your choice to remain a worker or to become an achiever.

Types of Successful People

Each of us is one of these persons: an achiever or a succeeder. Those whom I call a Victor in Success are discussed below:

Achievers

I define achievers as people who are living their life in a way to get possessions. They live in comfort but they don't accumulate wealth. They don't think of using their income to go into something new that will enlarge their financial territory. They earn to satisfy their needs and wants. They don't want to or think of investing in order to get a larger income.

There are people whose goals in life are limited to just getting a degree, having a good job, earning a living and taking care of their personal and household expenses. They are comfortable as long as all is going well. They don't think of becoming an employer one day. Their

Sacrificing For Success

minds are limited to just having a job and working to earn a salary for a positive living. They are blinded by their comfort.

I have realised that one way to enslave the mind of a human being is to give them a good job and pay them well. Then they are all yours, Mr Boss. Many people don't think of becoming their own boss. Think of becoming one.

Don't be enslaved by a comfort mentality. Use the little you earn to go further. If you're a good manager of a certain business, you make profit for the owners.

If, for example, you make a profit of R240000 for them after taking into consideration all the operational expenses and you get R16000 as your salary after tax and other deductions, you could save a little out of that R16000 to start your own business. You could save enough capital to start another business. Your sacrifice comes from squeezing all your expenses into the money left after saving for future investment.

After all, there are financial institutions and potential investors that are willing to invest in your business if you have a good convincing business plan. Think! Then you can become your own manager when you own your business. In addition, the growth continues when you become an employer. You can decide to work from a distance when your business has grown while you pursue other things. Then the profit comes to you. That is what I call success.

Sacrificing For Success

If all you do is to work to pay your expenses, your life won't be fruitful. Living on credit lets you enjoy now, but later you will be complaining that you have too many debts. You need to do something that is going to generate increased income. Consider generating larger income by sacrificing from the little that you have.

Succeeders

The second type of people whom I admire are succeeders. These are people who use the little income they receive to start something that will generate a larger income for them eventually. By investing or keeping a certain amount of their salary to start their own business or company, they follow a path for success. These people don't want to remain in their comfort zone.

They are employees who don't want to remain employees forever. They did not get educated to become employees. They became employees to get experience while they raise their own capital. Their own goal and dream is to become their own boss. They are eager to move from being an employee to being an employer. They are not extravagant in their spending because they buy only what is necessary, not whatever they want. They don't do any unnecessary luxurious shopping. They budget very well and avoid debts at all costs. They always preserve all that they have in order to achieve their goals in success. Their aim during their employment period is to raise enough capital to get to where they want to be in a given timeframe.

Sacrificing For Success

Principles of Success

If we want to go somewhere far in life, to reach an ultimate goal, we need to make sacrifices. We know that success requires sacrifice. This saying has become common knowledge. When planning your life and sacrifices to be made, here are the principles that I want you to follow:

- *You can be anything you want to be*
- *Time waits for no man*
- *Sacrifice to keep your life happy*
- *There is nothing you cannot do, be or have*
- *Nothing is worth the sacrifice if it doesn't make you happy*
- *Be yourself*
- *Anything you need is inside of you*
- *Only surround yourself with positive people*
- *Concentrate on what you want*

You can be anything you want to be

If you want a great life, you must commit to leading a great life. You must do things that many people don't do, for example, thinking like the minority not like the majority.

Time waits for no man

Time is money; time is precious and it controls your destiny. Any goal or life objective must be set to be achieved within a certain time frame. We are not going to live forever. We will be gone one day. It may be in 60 years, in 50 weeks or even next week. We can always

Sacrificing For Success

execute an action that will bring about the result we hope for if we are willing to sacrifice.

Sacrifice to keep your life happy

We should always embrace the fact that this life is short and unpredictable. Knowing this, we must live life to the fullest every day. Your obligation is to give your best shot to everything you do. It is the strategy to do your best in everything in order to give your great energy to your family and to everyone you encounter. Always leave the best of you in every moment.

If you were gone tomorrow, what would people say about you? What can you do that will leave a lasting positive memory in the lives of everyone who comes into contact with you?

The only things that matter are: how you made others feel and how you felt in your heart. It's about realising that your possessions will not go with you when you die. The spirit lives, but the things die with your physical body.

Remembering that you are going to die is the greatest reminder we can have in our daily lives because it keeps us focused on what is important and what is real. It helps us to sacrifice for important things that will keep us happy while we are still alive.

Sacrificing For Success

There is nothing you cannot do, be or have
With God all things are possible ~Luke1:37.

I can do everything Through Christ the Lord who enables me. ~ Phillipians4:13

If there has been someone who has achieved what you desire, you can achieve it too. This doesn't mean it will be easy, but it means it is possible. As long as it is possible you can walk towards it. You can come up with a strategy to make your dream a reality.

Learn what you need to do to live your craziest, abundant, happy life filled with joy, peace and happiness. It may be a life most people would consider impossible. Impossible, when broken down, states: "I'm possible". Impossible drives the procedure of making a strategy and being willing to work for that strategy.

Nothing is worth the sacrifice if it doesn't make you happy

If your dream won't make you happy or make you a better person, then don't make time for it. If it doesn't make you happy and better now while you're doing it or isn't going to make you happy as a result of doing it, then it is most likely not worth the effort. Anything that is worth doing is going to require a great fight with determination until it is done to win a great prize.

You will have to suffer and sacrifice for anything that is worthwhile in life. Ask yourself about anything you do or sacrifice for: Does it make me happy and better? Ask

10

Sacrificing For Success

yourself: Will this sacrifice lead to more happiness in the long term? If not, you should let it go.

Be yourself.

It is disheartening to see many people living a life they don't want to live and doing the things that they don't like doing just because they listened to other people who did the same. The only way you can live a happy life and be still more successful is by just being you. Be you! It is the most important thing you can apply to your life: "You be you". You will never be truly happy if you're not yourself and if you're constantly doing things to please other people, to compete with others or to be like another person.

You are unique. That's the greatest gift that God has given you. If you follow your own path regardless if it fits in with others, you can open up space for great things to enter your life. Compare your life with no one and compete with no one.

Creative men are not motivated by desire to beat others, but by the desire to achieve. ~ *Ayn Rand*.

Make your own decisions and it will lead to your best possible life.

Everything you need is inside of you

We see an endless number of people who seem to have it all materially, but they are empty inside and do not feel complete. Other people and things will never satisfy you. Russell Simmons says: "Needing nothing attracts everything".

Sacrificing For Success

When you come from a place of needing nothing outside of yourself and seeking nothing outside of yourself to make yourself happy, you're creating space for more amazing greater things to enter into your life. And, if things don't come, it is fine, for then you don't need them. Real happiness is never found outside of us. It is not found in possessions or wealth. Happiness is always and only found within us. It is the state of our mind. Happiness is the greatest level of success. Do what feels good; the rest will follow.

Surround yourself with positive people
A man who is always crying will not be heard~ African Proverb.

The reason why I choose few friends is because I do not like being with people who are negative in every circumstance they are in. I don't like people who are always negative-minded and those who always give excuses.

Don't make room for toxic people in your life. Only have space for positive-minded people. Surrounding yourself with zeal killers is one of the worst things you can do if you want live a fulfilled and successful life. Unfortunately, not everyone, including family members and friends, will share the same positive energy you have. In time, some will; some might never get to look on life positively. Let them run their own race and live their own life. You focus on living your own life and in making your dreams a reality. Focus on your own happiness. People who are truly aligned with you will never hold you back

Sacrificing For Success

from living the life you want to live. Don't ever dim your light to fit in with others. Shine your line bright to your maximum. Those who see the projection of your light waves will shine with you.

You cannot live a great life, a happy life, if you surround yourself with negative-minded people who always have excuses and oppose your ideas.

Concentrate on what you want

Whatever you want is what you must focus on. What you focus on is what you'll find. If you search for negativity in anything in this world, you will find it. If you search for hate, anger, violence and sadness, you will find it; but the same is true on the other side.

If your intention is to search for good, you'll find the good. Whatever meaning and interpretation you give it is what you'll have. Whatever meaning you give to your life, becomes your life. Students who look negatively on their study modules always seem to perform poorly. Negative minds produce negative results whereas positive minds produce positive results. Should your situation be considered a failure, a heartbreak or an opportunity to build your character? Focus on what you want. Bill Gates said, "Life is not fair; get used to it".

Your experience will make you stronger. There is no such thing as reality; we choose our own reality by the meaning we give to each moment of our lives. Make it your intention to look for the good in your life. Notice the good

Sacrificing For Success

in others and be grateful for what you have. See challenges as the opportunity to show your true character.

Remember that whatever you give your attention to will become your happenstance and experience in life. Practise seeing the good in your life and in others. Think of the best and expect the best. Always ask yourself how can this benefit my life? Live who you are, love who you are and look forward to who you will become.

Sacrificing For Success

Seven people you need to avoid

The reason you need to avoid these people is because they can be dangerous to your life, goals, and health. If you want to live a healthy and long successful achieving life, you need to avoid the following people:

Gossipers

People who talk about other people and criticise them to you are most likely to be talking about you in the same way. The only way to stop a gossip who is talking negatively about other people is to say, "I don't want to hear you talk about them like this". If you listen to gossips, you'll end up being part of the gossip or might even start to believe the negative things being said.

Many times the gossip is about the people you work with, your friend or family members. You have to stop the gossiper and help them understand the gossiping is not going to help anyone.

Jealous Haters

Anger causes trouble and a bad temper is like a flood, but who can stand when there is jealousy. ~ Proverbs 27:4

The second sort of people you should avoid are the "Jealous haters". Jealous people are usually people who want exactly what you have. They are people who want to devalue you by saying negative things about you. I also believe that criticism makes people do better, while haters makes you do things faster. However, don't let them dethrone you; don't allow them devalue who you are.

Sacrificing For Success

Understand that you are a child of God, and that you are here to do something special.

You ask how do I know if this person is jealous? and how do I deal with this hater? Well, usually when you tell them something good or worthwhile they:

- Try to shut you down automatically
- Try to overpower you
- Try to limit your courage
- Try to make you feel "not good enough"

Time wasters

Time wasters come in many different forms. You have to understand the type of time wasters you are dealing with. Some people love to bring things about. You have to ask them what the bottom line is. Some people love to talk about unimportant things like celebrity gossip, sports or anything that just wastes time. You have to shut them down and ask them to get to the point so that you can get on with your business.

Most time wasters are completely unaware that they are being wasteful and are not time conscious. They do not know how to manage the clock themselves and that makes them waste your time unintentionally. You have to shut them down and let them know that you have important things to do. You can tell them that you will get back to them another time.

Sacrificing For Success

Money Grabbers

Money grabbers are people who run away when it is time to pay the bill. These are people continually asking for things; people who just want to spend your money. How do you know if someone is a money grabber? Ask yourself, "Who grabs your money?" Am I buying things for this person to help or just buying because they are asking for them? Many times money grabbers will ask for things they do not even need and that is how you know it.

Overly sensitive People

Overly sensitive people are ones who come with a great deal of emotional baggage. These people have a thousand problems or more. Overly sensitive people are going to appear in your world. You should realise that they have no part in your life. Help them solve some problems, but do not try to solve all of their problems.

How do you know if someone is overly sensitive? They are always meticulous about their clothes and about their conversations. They always feel that they are being attacked. They are fussy about everything they do.

You have to understand that these people might be part of your life, but you don't have to spend too much of your time with them. Remember that you have big goals to accomplish.

Excuse-Makers

One thing that made it difficult for me to have friends in my university life is that I never liked excuse-makers. I always stick to plans. Excuse-makers are people who, if

Sacrificing For Success

you plan to do something with them, always come with many reasons why not to do it at that time or why they can't be there. Let us say you planned to study a certain module at a certain time. When the time arrives, they will tell you that it's going to be very cold today. I mean they don't even want to discover what is important in their life at a certain point.

People who always give excuses are not suitable to be in your life. Excuses are such statements as:

- I'm hungry
- I'm tired
- It's too cold or too hot
- I'm going to…
- I need to…
- I'm bored
- I'm broke

They have millions of excuses and they never want to act. They will always have excuses because they want you to join in their excuses.

I have seen successful people giving excuses too, so understand that excuse-makers come in different forms. You have to be willing to understand what their excuse is or what is missing in them. Then you can help that person or completely separate yourself from them.

Many people are always going to tell you why it won't work, why you shouldn't do it or why it can't happen

Sacrificing For Success

They are not willing to sacrifice and they will try to talk you out of your determination. Understand what they are really saying. Sometimes they might have fear for you, but that fear is illogical. Be able to understand it and dismiss it.

Miss-educated people

Yes, I do not mean uneducated people, but miss-educated people who have the wrong idea of what it takes to be successful. They may be highly educated people who have degrees, awards, experience and all kinds of training, but it doesn't mean that they know exactly what you have to do to be successful. Sometimes you have to watch out. There are sheep and wolves out there. Some friends are indirect enemies. Watch out for "frenemies". Determine who they are so that they will not talk you out of your journey to greatness.

Understand that some people are educated in social terms, but might not have common sense; they might not have wisdom or simple understanding. Watch out for people who will distract you from reaching your purpose.

However, there are some times when you cannot avoid these people. The best thing to do is to understand them and their intelligence. Be able to gather the intelligence that is necessary to make the right informed decisions.

Sacrificing For Success

Don't be Controlled by these Things

- *Your past*
- *Other people's opinions and judgements*
- *Limited beliefs you project upon yourself*
- *Relationships*
- *Money*

Some people are not living in the present because they are stuck in the muddy soil of their past. If you want to enter into greatness and be successful in life, don't be controlled by the following things:

Your past

Don't allow your past to control your present or your future life. Whatever has happened in your past you must let go. Leave the pain in your past behind so that it cannot block the light of your bright future. Your past is gone. Whatever happened, whether unjust, cruel, harsh, whatever the case, reliving the happenstance will never do you any good.

If someone did you wrong, the only way forward is that you must let go and move on. If you live in hate, they win. If you reside in the victim story, they win. If you want to win, you must focus on building your future.

Release the weight from your back so you can be free. Do not allow the events of your past, which are now gone, to ruin this perfect moment that God has offered you. Let go and live in joy, peace and happiness fully.

Sacrificing For Success

Other People's Opinions and judgements

Do not allow other people's opinions and judgements control the direction of your life. The need to fit in and be wanted can cause you to travel down paths you don't want to travel. Pleasing people is a curse that should be avoided at all costs. Before doing anything ask yourself, "Am I doing this because I want to or because of my fear of judgements from others if I don't?" You were born unique for a reason. You were born to stand out, to be appreciated and loved for who you are.

Don't dim your light so you can fit into the dull background of other people's lives. Shine your light as bright as you are and others who see your light will shine with you.

Limited beliefs you project upon yourself

Don't allow your life to be controlled by your own limited beliefs. These beliefs may be conscious, but more than likely, they are unconscious. There might be unconscious limitations that have been conditioned in you from when you were young and throughout your entire life by listening to those around you who never reached for their own dream. Notice your own limiting beliefs and tell them to shut up. There is nothing you cannot do, nothing you cannot have, and nothing that you cannot be as long as you believe in yourself. If you believe in yourself, trust in God and work as if everything depends on you.

When you change your beliefs from limited to unlimited, your potential becomes unlimited. Imagine what you could achieve if you live your life as if everything is

21

Sacrificing For Success

possible, as though miracles are standard requirements of everyday as the saying goes:

"When there is no enemy within, the enemy outside cannot do harm". *~ African Proverb.*

If you think you are too small to make a difference, then you haven't spent a night with a mosquito~ *African Proverb.*

When you have nothing inside that is holding you back, there is nothing outside that can hold you back either. Your entire life can change instantly when you decide to change your mindset and see adversity as a gift and see that by making a choice, every challenge is a blessing rather than a curse.

Relationships

If you always need to make another person happy to feel complete, then you are always one moment from a breakdown. That person may leave or become unhappy. The relationship you are in is really not going well.

I am not suggesting to you to avoid relationships. All I am saying is that there is no force on this earth greater than love and connection. I am talking about those who feel that they cannot live if they aren't in a relationship and those who will be with just anyone including the wrong ones to avoid spending a moment being single. You need to develop enough mental strength so that you get to the point where you don't need others to make you happy.

Sacrificing For Success

Then you are just as happy alone as you are in a relationship.

Money

Money is what controls majority of humans on this planet. This does not mean you shouldn't want abundance. It doesn't mean that money is evil, though it is the root of all evil. You know as well as I do what great things you can do and how many people can receive your charity when you have abundance of money.

However, do not allow your decisions to be controlled by money. If you choose something only on the factor of how much money is involved, you have made a big wrong decision. What you will find is that when you follow your heart and live with the intention to serve others, you will give it all your best every single day.

When you follow your intuition and truly give your soul, it is then that money will come in greater amount than if you work simply for the sake of chasing money. So, challenge yourself to live the kind of life you want to live, free from being controlled by anything. Find your freedom and fully live.

Sacrificing For Success

Put God First

Put God first means commit your plans to God so that He will make them successful. He alone can give you ideas and plans that will result in the kind of future you hope for. That's why he said:

I, the Lord your God, know the kind of plans I have towards you, to give you the kind of future you hope for. – *Jeremiah 29:11*.

Indeed, God the creator is not selfish. His plans are there to grant us our expectations and lead us into the kind of future we hope for. Put God first and everything will fall in place. Commit your plans to Him so that He can bless them and make them successful.

Trust in the Lord with all your heart; do not depend on your own understanding. Seek his will in all you do, and he will show you which path to take. - Proverbs 5:5-6(NLT)

Sacrificing For Success

Do not commit the following errors

1. Not planning your finances
2. Buying with consumer credit
3. Making just the minimum payment on your credit card
4. Not saving for retirement or financial freedom
5. Making financial decisions based on emotions
6. Focusing too much on money and neglecting the process
7. Not educating yourself financially

Error 1: Not planning your finances

Many people get their salary or wages and start paying their debts and still hope that they have enough money left until the end of the month. By planning your savings, living expenses, avoiding overspending and by following a financial budget, you can have control over your finances.

Many people do not have a clue about where their money is going and always have little left over at the end of the month. Check your account every day for the next 30 days. It might not be pretty, but you will be conscious in ensuring where your money is coming from and where actually it is going. It will help you. It will help you in knowing whether you should buy those R500 sunglasses or not? When you actively manage your money, you become better at it and it gives you the experience to manage more money.

Error 2: Buying with consumer credit

There are a few benefits in using a credit card. Building a credit history is important. Many cards have protection insurance, cash back and other benefits. However, if a credit card is not used correctly, it will affect your financial life very badly.

I am a retail manager in making and I should know. This is because credit cards encourage people to spend more money than they have. You can have R1000 in your pocket and be able to spend the R1000, but with credit cards you don't have to pay the full amount right away. The credit card makes it easier for you to break your budget by spending beyond your limit.

Not planning your finances can lead to overspending which is financially dangerous. This is because credit cards charge interest at rates that vary from 8% to 30% per year.

Error 3: Making Just Minimum Payments on your credit cards

Let's say you have a credit card with a debt of R5000 with an interest rate of 16% and you made a minimum payment of R50 since you don't want to spend much from your salary or income. The problem is that you haven't done the math before making the payment. Therefore, you don't realise that the interest alone is R67 (R5000 times one-twelfth of 16% annual interest). It is added to your debt. Even though you do pay some of your debt, it keeps growing which means that your interest cost gets higher. Eventually you'll find yourself with much debt that you cannot handle. The average credit interest rate for consumer spending is 15%.

Sacrificing For Success

So let's say that there is R1000 debt in your credit card with a minimum payment of R50. You get charged R12.50 for paying only a minimum payment of R50. The following month you will owe R962.50 if you haven't charged anything more. If you always make the minimum payment, you will be paying the original debt plus the cost of interest on the previous interest charges. This is called compound interest and will result in your paying the R1000 at R50 a month over 20 months plus 3 to 4 more months at R50 to pay for the interest. If you make only a minimum payment of R15 each month, it will take 12 years to pay it off and the total interest you will pay is R1,163.43. If you continue to charge purchases to your credit card and just pay the minimum each month, eventually your debt will exceed the limit on your card and the credit card company will stop you from using the card. Therefore, avoid making minimum payments.

Error 4: Not saving for retirement or financial freedom

Many people save money, but they save it for the wrong reasons. Very few people save money for retirement or for financial freedom. You might be able to produce income now, but you might not be able to do it forever. Life is so unpredictable. You cannot leave it to the government or your children to provide for your social security. Your retirement and financial freedom are your responsibility. Even if you don't earn much, a little bit of saving does count, especially if you invest smartly and get compound interest within the investment.

Sacrificing For Success

If you put only R10,000 in an investment account offering 7% compound interest, in 37 years' time you'll have R132,298 If, in addition, you deposit R100 each month, you'll have R343,176. This is enough to start something that will earn you a living. It pays to invest. The earlier you start, the better it is.

Error 5: Making Financial Decisions based on Emotions

Making money decisions based on emotions can put you in a very vulnerable position. This is simply because when we are in our emotional state, we are not rational in our thinking and we can make mistakes. These can be positive or negative emotions. If you are happy and optimistic, you think of great ways you can make cash such as investing and still think critically and logically.

On the negative side, we get to complain of things we spend too much on. Avoid making important decisions while emotional. Wait and use intelligence and rationality.

Think of Steve Jobs. In his anger when he was fired by Apple he sold all his ownership in the company. He got few shares back, worth $1.8 million, but if he had avoided taking the decision in his anger, he would have kept $6.6 million in his possession. Don't let anger make you take permanent financial decisions that you will regret later.

Sacrificing For Success

Error 6: Focusing too much on money and neglecting the process

Many successful people like Patrice Motsepe (one of the richest black persons in South Africa) and many more have this philosophy. If you are to be successful, you need to love the process and you have to be passionate. As the saying goes:

"If you go into business only to make money, you're better off doing nothing". When you focus on the money and neglect the process, you'll end up losing. For example, if you have a business, but are unwilling to create a relationship with your customers, you cannot make quick sales. You will be missing out on a lifetime of making your business successful by neglecting that process.

Error 7: Not educating yourself financially
He that loves to learn loves Knowledge~ King Solomon.

He that learns teaches~ African proverb

Money management is not something that is taught at school. The majority of our parents were not wealthy. Therefore, learning about personal finance and how to manage your money is your own responsibility. Neglecting this area will keep you uneducated and therefore less likely to become financially independent.

Sacrificing For Success

Are you living the life you want?

I want to ask you a question. *Are you living the life you want to live?* Everyone has his or her dream life. We all have a picture in our mind of that life we want to live. My question is simple: are you currently living that life? Most people would say, "No". Well, why not? The answer is often somewhere close to:

- It seems impossible
- It is hard
- It is not feasible
- I have zero confidence
- I lack resources
- I don't know

Now let me ask you another question: *Have you actually tried achieving the life you want to live?* Most persons would say, "Yes".

In my case, I do it every day. That is what my job or education is for. These are the little steps I take every single day to reach my goals.

Let me ask the same question a little bit differently: *Have you tried your hardest in achieving that life? Have you given your best shot?* Most people fall silent and do not answer.

They don't want to say "No" and appear weak or sound like a failure.

Sacrificing For Success

They don't want to say "Yes" because they know deep inside that it would be a lie.

They haven't tried their best.

Now another question for you if you're a brother: *Have you tried your hardest in achieving that life, as hard as you have tried getting a girl?*

If you think about it, the answer is "No". However, your determination to get a girl is phenomenal. You are texting to different girls on Facebook, Whatsapp, and Twitter, etc. every single day. You don't care who they are! You don't know whether they're in a relationship or not, whether they want to talk to you or not. You're chatting with girls you haven't even seen. You don't even know if it's a girl and yet you're investing your time all night and day chatting with that person who has a picture of pretty Hazel.

However, notice the amount of hope you need in doing that; it's almost insane. There is no guarantee that any of those girls will date you, even if you try every single day. You're being rejected by a girl you have not even met.

If nine out ten don't message back or accept your request, you have already failed 90% of your task. That doesn't discourage you. You keep on trying.

Look at the amount of will and determination inside of you. However, just imagine for a second, if you saved all that time and put all that hope and will to work for

Sacrificing For Success

yourself not to find a hot girl, not to find the love of your life, but just to develop yourself. Imagine what you could accomplish.

Do you know why many girls befriend guys? It is for emotional support. Whenever they need help or have a problem in their life, whenever they need motivation or inspiration, they call you and you put your work aside and invest all your time and energy in motivating them, solving their problems, reassuring them and mostly doing their work. Then, when they are happy and need someone to hang out with, they go to their boyfriend, not you.

The moment a girl needs sex, she goes to her boyfriend, not you. Her boyfriend is her first priority, but the moment she gets depressed and needs someone to help her with her work, she thinks of you. You're using all the positivity inside of you to make someone else become successful. Why? Every time her boyfriend is busy, she texts you to keep herself busy. She's using you for her emotional support. She doesn't even think about you when she doesn't need you.

I know guys who spent hours texting with a girl chosen at random, guys who have been obsessed with some girl for years. Some are guys who haven't been with their ex-girlfriend in years. Some are guys who have literally become drivers for girls so they could spend time with them. Some are guys taking extreme pain to solve a girl's problem in the hope that she will fall in love with them. Some are guys who gave their time in a relationship and hardly thought about their careers. Some are guys

Sacrificing For Success

painstakingly trying to fix girls who voluntarily seek destruction and constantly invite trouble in their lives.

What are you getting in return? Nothing! These girls are not even dating you. If a girl wanted to date you, she would have dated you. It doesn't matter that she's dating someone else. When she is bored and her boyfriend is busy, she texts you to pass her time. There are some guys who volunteer willingly to become a "time pass" for girls. They have knowingly pushed themselves into the position where they are getting nothing except for the pleasure of chatting with a girl. Is that what your life is really all about?

Is this grand gift of life from God with all its innumerable possibilities and opportunities narrowed down to this? Chatting with some randomly selected girl! More than half of these girls are already dating someone. Why are you even chatting with them in the first place? "Oh, I chat with her because she's my friend, not because I want to have sex with her"!

Really! Do you also text with your male friends just as much as you do with her? Brothers, you need to stop this. You need to stop it right now. There are about 7,000,000,000 people in this world. Why are you letting one of them ruin your life?

No more excuses. You have to stop throwing away your entire potential in chasing some girl you have found at random. Decide now and commit to success. If you are obsessed with some girl, get over it right now. If you are

Sacrificing For Success

obsessed with your ex, get over it now. If some chick calls you when she needs help and you know that she is toying with you, get her out of your life right now.

You may ask, why? Why should I do this? As if, changing your life isn't important enough! Nevertheless, I will still give you reasons why:

Reason 1: Self-Esteem

If you send friend requests and messages to girls at random, how do you ever find out why they rejected you? Do you know why she "friend zoned" you and never dated you while she got herself a new boyfriend? You will never know. However, one thing that is definitely going to happen is that all this rejection will have a serious impact on your self-esteem. It is an impact that you mostly certainly don't need and don't deserve because the reason why she rejected you is based on her opinion of you.

She has nothing to do with your reality, so protect your self-esteem. Don't hand it to some person who would crush it because she would rather date a boy who depends on his daddy's money for cars, booze and parties. You don't need this unnecessary rejection in your life.

Reason 2: Achievement Is Better

What is a greater feeling than that of love? It is the feeling of achievement. Unlike love, the feeling of achievement is much better and permanent. It will last until the day you die. You may have regrets about your love life, but you will mostly regret not doing what you wanted to do in your life when you had the chance.

Sacrificing For Success

Reason 3: Money

Money gives you a better lifestyle; it gives you better options and it also gives you the freedom to do whatever you want. Forget about your sex life for a year or two, or however long it takes you to be successful; when you become successful, you will get the prettiest girls in the world, if you want that. Girls don't care about how you look or what personality you have. All they are looking for is a guy who is earning five times more than they are. Why? Because girls are attracted to successful guys. It is not a mystery. Sacrifice for success.

Reason 4: Self-Development

This is the most important reason: Put all that energy into building yourself and change your entire life. Then you can also change the lives of the people around you.

Reason 5: Help Others

When was the last time you spent money on a girl? Perhaps you spent it on dinners, movies, lunches, gifts, shopping or even to recharge her phone so you can talk to her?

When was the last time you spent any money on your mother? When was the last time you bought her a gift or even recharged her phone? When was the last time you took your mother out for dinner? Compare the amount of money you spent on a girl who is not even your girlfriend to how much you spent on your parents. Stop investing your money on relationships that have not even started. Use the money you have to change the lives of people around you, your parents, your brothers and sisters,

Sacrificing For Success

someone who needs help rather than buying a diamond necklace or clothes for a girl you hardly know. You can pay for someone's school fees or university application fee.

Those are the five reasons why you need to sit back for a moment, take some time and think really about how much time, money, and energy you have wasted in some meaningless pursuits. Work to make your goals a reality. Sacrifice to make your future bright.

You Need To:
Recognise the insane dedication with which you pursue those relationships every day and shift your attention from girls to self-betterment.

Acknowledge that you have your own dreams and that no one else is going to help you achieve them.

You are on your own.

Success requires sacrifice.

Sacrifice for success!

Sacrificing For Success

Thank you for buying and reading this book. Most important of all, there is information in my other books I've written especially for you. All the details on how you can get any of my books is written at the back of this book.

Follow me on Facebook: Author Blessed Thabang Mobosi

If you don't sacrifice for what you want, what you want becomes the sacrifice of what you don't want ~ Unknown

By the end of the year you will wish you had started earlier. It is not easy, but the result is worthwhile.

Whenever you don't feel like making the sacrifice, whether it is studying, investing, etc., remind yourself why you should.

Dedication + Determination = Distinction

The only way to get distinctions is to study almost every day.

Trust in God, but live as if everything depends on you.

If you're not living to make your dreams a reality, you will work to help someone else make theirs a reality.

SUCCESS IS NO ACCIDENT. IT IS HARD WORK, PERSEVERANCE, LEARNING, STUDYING, SACRIFICE AND MOST OF ALL, LOVE OF WHAT YOU ARE DOING.

Quotling.com

Source: Qoutling.com

Sacrificing For Success

Books by Blessed Thabang Mobosi

1. Destiny is a Matter of Choice
2. The Power of Determination
3. Steps to Success (A Key to Success Creativity)
4. The Crave Of the Youth
5. Fornication vs. Adultery. Sex Before Marriage
6. The Voice of Revolution (A Poetry Anthology)
7. A Life Partner
8. Sacrificing for Success

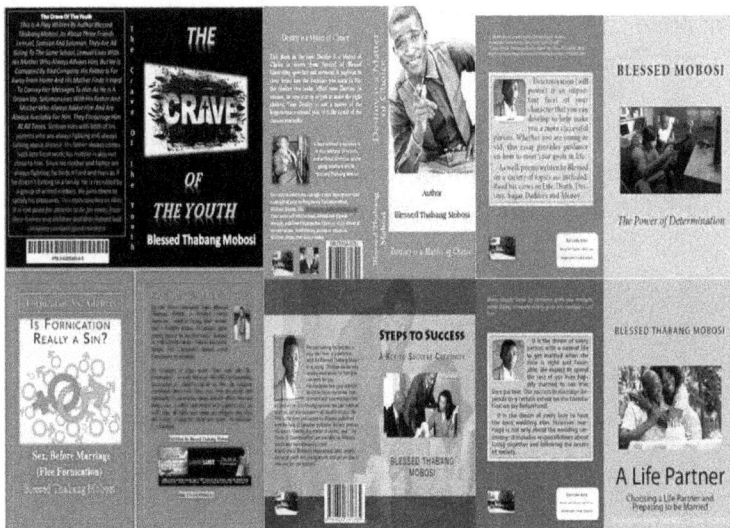

Sacrificing For Success

To order any of the books

Email: Blessed.btm@gmail.com

Facebook Page: Author Blessed Thabang Mobosi
Website: http://amazon.com/author/blessedmobosi
Cell: +27 61 953 9726
+27 78 506 5555
+27 72 875 6983
+27 64 337 1725

Download the Kindle version or order a printed paperback copy on Amazon.com.

Type the name of the book or author on the search bar at amazon.com or takealot.com or just search for Author Blessed Thabang Mobosi to see different options you can choose.

www.ingramcontent.com/pod-product-compliance
Lightning Source LLC
Chambersburg PA
CBHW071436040426
42445CB00012BA/1374